MIRACLE LANDING
ON THE HUDSON

S.L. HAMILTON

A&D Xtreme
An imprint of Abdo Publishing
abdobooks.com

abdobooks.com

Published by Abdo Publishing, a division of ABDO, PO Box 398166, Minneapolis, Minnesota 55439. Copyright © 2020 by Abdo Consulting Group, Inc. International copyrights reserved in all countries. No part of this book may be reproduced in any form without written permission from the publisher. A&D Xtreme™ is a trademark and logo of Abdo Publishing.

Printed in the United States of America, North Mankato, MN.
092019
012020

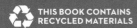

Editor: John Hamilton
Copy Editor: Bridget O'Brien
Graphic Design: Sue Hamilton & Dorothy Toth
Cover Design: Victoria Bates
Cover Photo: AP
Interior Photos & Illustrations: Airport K9/Brian Edwards-pg 6; AP-pgs 1, 2-3, 10-11, 13, 18-19 & 27; Getty Images-pgs 28-29; iStock-pgs 12 & 14-15; Reuters-pgs 16-17, 20-21, 22-23, 24-25 & 26; Science Source-pgs 8-9; Shutterstock-pgs 7 & 30-31; Warner Bros-pgs 4-5 & 32.

Library of Congress Control Number: 2019905466
Publisher's Cataloging-in-Publication Data

Names: Hamilton, S.L., author.
Title: Miracle landing on the Hudson / by S.L. Hamilton
Description: Minneapolis, Minnesota : Abdo Publishing, 2020 | Series: Xtreme rescues | Includes online resources and index.
Identifiers: ISBN 9781532190049 (lib. bdg.) | ISBN 9781644943526 (pbk.) | ISBN 9781532175893 (ebook)
Subjects: LCSH: US Airways Flight 1549 Crash Landing, Hudson River, N.Y. and N.J., 2009--Juvenile literature. | Aircraft accidents--Juvenile literature. | Aircraft bird strikes--Juvenile literature. | Airplane crash survival--Juvenile literature. | Sullenberger, Chesley, 1951---Juvenile literature.
Classification: DDC 363.12409--dc23

CONTENTS

IN THE HUDSON RIVER

US Airways Flight 1549 took off from LaGuardia Airport in New York on Thursday, January 15, 2009, at 3:41 p.m. The Airbus A320 was full, with 150 passengers and 5 flight crew members headed for Charlotte, North Carolina. After a normal takeoff, the jet quickly reached 3,200 feet (975 m).

A flock of Canada geese struck the plane just 54 seconds after takeoff. Captain Chesley B. Sullenberger III, nicknamed "Sully," and First Officer Jeffrey Skiles heard and felt a loud explosion. Flames erupted from the plane's two engines. The smell of burning feathers and fuel filled the cabin. Both engines lost thrust. The pilots knew the plane was going down fast.

XTREME FACT

Flight 1549 dropped at a rate of 18 feet per second (5.5 m per second). Without either engine, the plane would crash in less than 3 minutes.

Bird Strikes

Airports use many methods to keep birds away. Food that attracts them, such as grass or garbage, is kept to a minimum. Gunshots, loud bangs, and distress calls scare away birds. Handlers bring dogs to chase flocks of birds on the ground. Birds of prey, both real and robots, take to the skies to clear the area.

Piper the border collie works with his handler, Brian Edwards, to chase away ducks, geese, and snowy owls from a Michigan airport.

Pilots are trained to deal with bird strikes. Most bird strikes result in little or no damage to planes. Some may cause an engine to fail. Usually, one engine is enough to get a plane safely back to an airport. However, sometimes a plane is so damaged that it crashes.

A golden eagle is used to chase away seagulls and other birds at an airport in Europe.

AIRP

XTREME FACT

There are about 13,000 bird strikes each year in the United States, but most of these accidents end safely.

Double Engine Failure

Captain Sullenberger and First Officer Skiles knew that both engines were out after the bird strike. They immediately began emergency actions. Sully radioed LaGuardia Airport to let them know the plane was trying to return. Air traffic controller Patrick Harten aided Sully by clearing runways at LaGuardia and nearby Teterboro Airport in New Jersey. But then came the unforgettable words from Captain Sullenberger, "We can't do it. We're gonna be in the Hudson."

Both of Flight 1549's engines failed after the plane encountered a flock of Canada geese.

BRACE FOR IMPACT

The only smooth place that was long, wide, and clear enough to land the Airbus was the Hudson River. Captain Sullenberger lined up the plane with the river. It cleared the 1,600-foot (488-m) -high George Washington Bridge with less than 1,000 feet (305 m) to spare. Sully came on the intercom and told the flight attendants, "Brace for impact."

"Brace. Brace. Heads down. Stay down." —Flight attendants Sheila Dail and Donna Dent in the front and Doreen Welsh in the back of the plane chanted these instructions to the passengers.

A video still frame of Flight 1549 coming in to land on the Hudson River.

THE WORLD FINDS OUT

As he monitored the air speed, Captain Sullenberger lined up the plane with the nose up 11 degrees and the wings level. The Airbus landed on the Hudson River and slid across the water to a stop. A miracle had occurred: the plane was mostly intact.

Hundreds of calls began pouring into 911 to report a plane had just landed in the Hudson River. Ferries, helicopters, police, ambulances, and divers all raced to the scene of the downed plane. The news media was there within minutes.

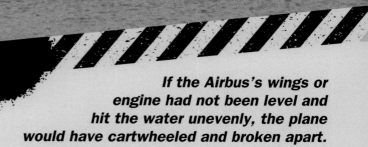

US Airways Flight 1549 after landing on the Hudson River.

XTREME FACT

If the Airbus's wings or engine had not been level and hit the water unevenly, the plane would have cartwheeled and broken apart.

GET OUT OR DROWN

Captain Sullenberger landed safely, but there was a break in a section by the tail. Freezing-cold water began to fill the cabin of the plane. The Hudson River was coming in and people were at risk of drowning. Sully told the flight attendants and passengers, "Evacuate."

Flight attendants Sheila Dail and Donna Dent opened the exit doors at the front of the plane. One passenger in the back opened the rear emergency exit door. Instead of helping, water began flooding in faster. Flight attendant Doreen Welsh tried to close it twice, but couldn't. She directed everyone in back to get to the front of the plane, even if they had to climb over the seats. People stayed calm, but everyone knew they had to get out or drown.

Wings, Rafts & Water

Passengers hurried to escape the sinking plane. Some walked onto the plane's wings. Others slid onto escape rafts. A few people slipped or jumped off the plane and ended up swimming in the Hudson River.

The air temperature that January day was only 20 degrees Fahrenheit (-7°C). People in the Hudson were swimming in water that was only 40 degrees Fahrenheit (4°C). Hypothermia was suddenly the survivors' greatest threat.

Captain Sullenberger was the last person off the plane. He moved up and down the length of the plane calling, "Is anyone there? Come forward."

BOAT RESCUES

Sully landed the plane across from the New York Waterways' ferry terminal. Ferries were waiting for the evening rush hour. It only took about four minutes for the first ferry, the *Thomas Jefferson*, to reach the plane. Soon more boats arrived to help.

As the passengers and crew moved out of the plane's cabin, the deck hands prepared to help rescue them. Ferry boat decks are 7 feet (2 m) above the water. They are not designed for rescue. Luckily, the boats carried nets and rope ladders that allowed people to climb up to the deck.

RESCUE DIVERS

The New York Police Department Scuba Team arrived by helicopter. Divers plunged into the icy-cold water to assist the passengers who had jumped or fallen in the Hudson. Although people can survive for 30 minutes to 1 hour in freezing water, they experience hypothermia in a matter of minutes. The swimming passengers had difficulty thinking, or making their arms and legs move. The rescue divers were quickly there to help.

AID STATIONS

Ambulances and aid stations were set up on the New York and New Jersey shores. Most passengers had signs of mild hypothermia. They were given blankets, dry clothing, and hot drinks. If they needed additional help, they were brought by waiting ambulances to local hospitals.

A Flight 1549 passenger is given a blanket and assistance by emergency personnel on shore.

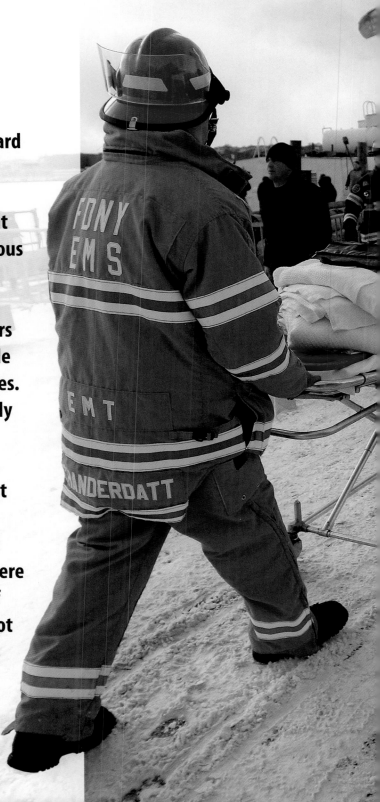

ALL 155 RESCUED

Of the 155 people on board Flight 1549, only five people sustained major injuries. Flight attendant Doreen Welsh had a serious gash on her leg when a metal bar came through the floor. First responders treated four other people with more serious injuries. Most passengers had only minor wounds or mild hypothermia. Captain Sullenberger did not rest until he knew everyone was safe. It took several hours because people were brought to both sides of the shore. When Sully got word that everyone was rescued, the miracle was complete.

First responders bring in stretchers and supplies to the New York shoreline near where Flight 1549 landed on the Hudson River.

XTREME FACT

Doreen Welsh's leg injury resulted in a redesign of one of the Airbus's beams. Today's planes have less chance of a metal bar breaking into the cabin area during a ditching or gear-up landing.

RECOVERING THE PLANE

The empty Airbus floated down the Hudson River. The strong currents and ice made it difficult to pull it out of the water. The plane was finally recovered on January 17, 2009.

The crew of US Airways Flight 1549, from left to right: flight attendant Donna Dent, First Officer Jeffrey Skiles, Captain Chesley "Sully" Sullenberger III, and flight attendants Doreen Welsh and Sheila Dail.

The data recovery and cockpit voice recorder were reviewed by the National Transportation Safety Board. They called the flight "the most successful ditching in aviation history." The five crew members were awarded the Master's Medal of the Guild of Air Pilots and Air Navigators. New York City's Mayor Michael Bloomberg also awarded keys to the city to the flight crew, calling them "five real American heroes."

WHAT IF IT HAPPENS TO YOU?

To survive a plane ditching in the water, follow these steps:

1) Stay calm. This is the most important thing to do in all survival situations.

2) Follow the flight crew's directions. They train to know what to do during disasters.

3) Stay dry for as long as you can. A wet body loses heat quickly.

4) If in the water, look for the fastest way out. Hypothermia makes it difficult for a person to think or move normally.

5) Once out of the water, take off wet clothing and put on something dry. Get medical help.

Boats surround the empty Flight 1549 Airbus.

GLOSSARY

AIR TRAFFIC CONTROLLER
A person trained to direct aircraft with landings and takeoffs at airports. They keep track of every aircraft's speed, position, and altitude (distance from the ground) in a specific area.

AIRBUS A320
A type of plane designed to carry a large number of passengers on shorter, regularly-scheduled flights.

BIRDS OF PREY
Birds that eat meat, such as eagles, hawks, falcons, and owls. They have sharp talons and hooked beaks for grasping and tearing at prey.

DITCHING
An aircraft's forced landing on water during an emergency.

FERRY
A boat that transports people a short distance, usually from one city to another nearby city, and runs on a regular schedule. Many ferries run during morning and afternoon rush hours.

Today, the Flight 1549 Airbus is at the Carolinas Aviation Museum in Charlotte, North Carolina.

First Responders
People such as police, firefighters, ambulance drivers, emergency medical technicians (EMTs), and paramedics, who are the first on the scene of an emergency situation.

Hypothermia
When a person's body temperature drops below 95 degrees Fahrenheit (35°C). Mild hypothermia causes shivering and confusion. Severe hypothermia can cause a person's heart to stop, resulting in death.

Intercom
A system which allows someone speaking into a microphone to be heard on a speaker by people in a different room or area.

Rush Hour
A time when many people are coming and going from their homes to their work, and back to their homes, usually on Monday through Friday. Morning rush hour is 6 to 10 a.m. Evening rush hour is 4 to 8 p.m.

Thrust
The force that moves a plane through the air. Thrust is created by a plane's engines.

Online Resources

Booklinks
NONFICTION NETWORK
FREE! ONLINE NONFICTION RESOURCES

To learn more about the miracle landing on the Hudson, visit abdobooklinks.com or scan this QR code. These links are routinely monitored and updated to provide the most current information available.

INDEX